DARK PART OF THE FOREST

Tammy Ryan

BROADWAY PLAY PUBLISHING INC
New York
www.broadwayplaypublishing.com
info@broadwayplaypublishing.com

DARK PART OF THE FOREST
© Copyright 2006 by Tammy Ryan

First printing: July 2011
I S B N: 978-0-88145-500-7

Book design: Marie Donovan
Page make-up: Adobe Indesign
Typeface: Palatino
Printed and bound in the U S A

ABOUT THE AUTHOR

Tammy Ryan's plays have been produced and developed across the country at such theaters as The Alliance Theater Company, Florida Stage, People's Light and Theater Company, The Pittsburgh Playhouse, City Theater Company and elsewhere. Her writing for young audiences has twice won the National Playwriting for Youth Bonderman Award for THE GIFT OF THE PIRATE QUEEN (2007) and THE MUSIC LESSON (1999) which has received over twenty-five productions and was awarded the American Alliance of Theater in Education's Distinguished Play Award. Other plays include PIG (29th Street Rep), THE BOUNDARY (University of Pittsburgh Repertory Theater), IN THE SHAPE OF A WOMAN, BABY'S BLUES (also published by Broadway Play Publishing Inc), F B I GIRL: HOW I LEARNED TO CRACK MY FATHER'S CODE, A CONFLUENCE OF DREAMING (The REP) and LOST BOY FOUND IN WHOLE FOODS (Premiere Stages, Playwrights Theater of New Jersey) Awards include the Pittsburgh Cultural Trust's Creative Achievement Award, The Heinz Endowment's Creative Heights Grant and fellowships from the Pennsylvania Council on the Arts and the Sewanee Writers Conference.

A workshop of DARK PART OF THE FOREST was presented as an Independent Artist Project of the Hamburg Studio Artist Showcase Program at City Theater (Mark Masterson, Artistic Director) on 7 January 2000. The cast and creative contributors were:

JOAN..Nancy Bach
BILL.. Robert DiDonato
EMILY/STACY/YOUNG JOAN
.... Megan Mackenzie Lawrence
KAREN .... Bryn Jameson
HUNTER/WOODCUTTER/BOY......................Aaron Stetzik

Director.. Brenda Harger
Scenic design... Stephanie Miller
Sound design...Elizabeth Atkinson
Lighting design ....Gianni Downs
Costume design...Cheryl Young
Stage manager...Margie Romero

DARK PART OF THE FOREST was a winner of the 2006 Premiere Stages Playwriting Festival and received its world premiere at Premiere Stages, the professional theater-in-residence at Kean University (John Wooten, Artistic Director) on 16 July 2006. The cast and creative contributors were:

JOAN..Toby Posner
BILL..Gregory Northrop
EMILY/STACY/YOUNG JOAN ....Sarah Hyland
KAREN .... Rita Rehn
HUNTER/WOODCUTTER ....Joe Zehnder
BOY ....Jonathan Weisbrod

Director...John Wooten
Scenic design... Bill Motyka
Sound design... Christopher Bailey
Lighting design ....Nadine Charlsen
Costume design...Karen Lee Hart
Stage manager.. Dale Smallwood
Casting director .... Carol Hanzel

CHARACTERS & SETTING

JOAN, *38, wife and mother and aspiring writer*

BILL, *40, her air traffic controller husband*

EMILY, *13, their only daughter*

KAREN, *36,* JOAN's *best friend*

STACEY MOSKOWITZ, *murdered by Son of Sam in 1977, here she is a dead girl in* JOAN's *imagination, played by* EMILY

YOUNG JOAN, *16, as* JOAN *remembers her, played by* EMILY

Non speaking roles:

DARK FIGURE/HUNTER, *a man in the woods, appearing at first in reality, then recurring in* JOAN's *imagination as* THE WOODCUTTER *and* SON OF SAM. *Can be doubled by* BILL.

DARK FIGURE/BOY, *17,* JOAN's BOYFRIEND *from 1977. This actor can also double as* HUNTER.

A new house, built in the woods, west of Pittsburgh

*Time: Early October to the winter solstice 1999
And the summer of 1977 in* YOUNG JOAN's *memory.*

PROLOGUE:

(At rise: A clearing surrounded by forest, dark and impenetrable. Somewhere above the forest are stars. Lights begin to filter sunlight, sounds of birds and small animals. A swing hanging from a tree branch swings gently.)

JOAN: Once upon a time as a blue moon rose over a city near three rivers, a man, a woman and their little girl sleep, nestled amidst the black rolling hills that ran along the edge of the water, linked by bridges that span but never connect. The girl grew to be very beautiful and when she began to look at the world with wide doe eyes, the man and the woman moved away from the city, to the country, to the very heart of the dark, surrounding woods.

(Lights fade.)

Scene One

(In the darkness the sound of three car doors slamming, one after the other. As light rise:)

(JOAN stands looking at the house, a laptop over her shoulder. BILL enters carrying boxes. EMILY trails behind, carrying a backpack and large stuffed animal)

BILL: Still like it?

JOAN: I love it. And I love you.

BILL: If only I knew. All I had to do was build you a house in the country.

JOAN: That's not all…but it's a start.

(EMILY *drops her backpack with a thud.*)

EMILY: It took two hours to get here!

JOAN: That's because there was traffic.

BILL: Took one year, if you count from when we started building.

EMILY: She said it would take forty-five minutes from Pittsburgh. It has never taken forty-five minutes!

JOAN: I have driven here in forty-five minutes, when there's no traffic.

EMILY: In your imagination.

BILL: Emily.

EMILY: There's never *no* traffic.

BILL: There was an accident in the tunnel. That's not going to happen every day. On a good day it takes an hour.

JOAN: Not even. Besides it's beautiful out here. Why would you want to go back to Pittsburgh?

EMILY: Because all my friends are there.

JOAN: You don't know how lucky you're gonna be growing up in the country.

EMILY: Now she's gonna tell me all about how she grew up in big bad New York City.

JOAN: No I'm not. I'm going to tell you to appreciate what you have.

EMILY: We're out in the middle of nowhere! There are no signs of civilization!

JOAN: *(To* BILL*)* How about you? Are you happy?

BILL: Are you kidding? Twenty minutes from the airport. Not having to take the parkway will add five years to my life. And my marriage. *(Looking at* JOAN, *who is looking at the house)* What is it?

JOAN: *(Smiling again)* I can't believe we live here. I feel like different people already. Can't you see me in there baking cookies already?

BILL: Wait till you wake up in the morning with sunlight pouring in through that skylight.

EMILY: Can we go in?

BILL: *(Grabs* EMILY, *wrestling her in a bear hug)* I thought we'd spend the first night out here, camping under the stars so we can get back to nature.

EMILY: *(Punching him, giggling)* Not funny, Dad.

*(*JOAN *turns away from their horseplay.)*

BILL: What's the matter, you don't like the outdoors? Come on, breathe in the fresh air. It's good for you.

EMILY: Yeah, till we find out we're living on a toxic waste dump.

JOAN: Emily. We are not living on a toxic waste dump.

BILL: She'll get used to it.

EMILY: Come on, Dad, open the door.

JOAN: Yeah, come on, I gotta pee.

BILL: Okay, open the door, madam, your dream house awaits.

JOAN: Gimme the key.

BILL: You don't have the key?

JOAN: No. You don't have the key?

BILL: No. I thought you took the key.

JOAN: I never had the key.

EMILY: I saw a key on the kitchen counter when we were leaving.

JOAN: And you didn't pick it up?

EMILY: How was I supposed to know it was the key to this house?

BILL: How's she gonna know that?

JOAN: I don't believe it.

EMILY: It's a sign we shouldn't move.

JOAN: It's a sign we should've hired movers, then the only thing we'd have to bring would be the key.

BILL: We're saving two thousand dollars moving ourselves.

EMILY: Yeah, cause we're house poor. *(Jumps on swing)*

BILL: We're not house poor.

JOAN: We might be after we buy furniture.

BILL: So, what do we do?

EMILY: Let's go back home.

JOAN: This is home.

BILL: We have to go back to get the key.

JOAN: Pick the lock.

BILL: And then pay a hundred dollars to get it fixed? Besides I can't pick a lock.

JOAN: I might be able to. *(Looks in her purse, walks to door)*

BILL: Your mother, the New Yorker.

JOAN: *(Tries picking the lock)* Your father, the whimp.

BILL: We need the key.

JOAN: Then let's go, so we can get back before it gets dark.

BILL: Okay, but we can't leave everything out in the open.

JOAN: It'll be all right.

BILL: Someone might steal it.

JOAN: Who? There's nobody out here, but deer.

EMILY: Those thievin deer.

BILL: I'd feel more comfortable if someone stayed behind and watched the stuff.

(Sound: An airplane flies in low and loud)

JOAN: What are we, right on final?

BILL: No, we're not, he's busting noise abatement for some reason. Don't worry, that's not gonna happen a lot.

EMILY: Until one falls on us.

BILL: That's not gonna happen either.

EMILY: It already happened to those people in Hopewell Township.

BILL: We're not in Hopewell Township and that plane crashed in a ravine, where there weren't any people.

EMILY: Except for the people on the plane.

BILL: Emily, anywhere you live, a plane is flying over you. I'll make sure they vector over somebody else's house.

JOAN: I'll stay. Now that I'm finally here, I'm not going back.

BILL: *(To EMILY)* You wanna go back with me or stay with Mom?

EMILY: I don't want to stay here; it's boring.

JOAN: Fine. I couldn't take another two hours of her whining anyway.

EMILY: Can we get pizza at Napoli's! *(Pronounced "NAH-poh-lees)*

BILL: *(Stacking boxes)* There's a flashlight somewhere.

JOAN: You'll be back before dark. An hour there, if you speed.

BILL: Oh, now you want me to speed.

JOAN: Yes, I do. And come right back.

EMILY: But I'm *hungry*.

JOAN: Okay, but eat it in the car.

BILL: There won't be any traffic on the way back.

EMILY: So it'll only take forty-five minutes, right?

BILL: I'll stay. Emily and I will stay. You drive.

(BILL throws JOAN the car keys.)

EMILY: No!

JOAN: No. It's a gorgeous Indian Summer day. Not many of those left. I'll pee in the bushes, then I'll explore. What do we have two acres? Maybe I'll meet the neighbors.

BILL: You're here to watch the stuff.

JOAN: All right, I won't go anywhere. I'll start my novel, how's that?

EMILY: MA! *(Whispering)* Look a deer!!

JOAN: Oh look. Oh my god, it's staring right at us.

BILL: Get outta here!

JOAN: It's not afraid.

EMILY: She's beautiful.

JOAN: I thought they'd be afraid.

BILL: This is Pennsylvania, there are so many of them, they're fearless. *(He picks up a rock.)*

JOAN: Don't throw a rock at it. Wait, there it goes.

EMILY: Great. Wildlife. Any bears out here?

BILL: Yeah, that's right and mountain lions. Let's go.

(BILL *puts his arm around* EMILY, *leading her off growling, as* EMILY *giggles.)*

JOAN: *(Calling after them)* Save me some pizza!

BILL: *(Digs in his pocket and tosses a bag to her)* Here's a bag of peanuts. Don't say I don't care. And turn your cell phone on.

(They exit. A moment later, BILL *returns.* JOAN *holds out the keys, then pulls them away, teasing, he grabs her, takes the keys.)*

BILL: Thank you. What?

JOAN: Pick up a bottle of wine. The liquor store is right down the block from Napoli's. Maybe tonight—after Emily goes to sleep, we can start a fire…

BILL: *(Chuckles)* Too bad, it's not the old days, when I could run her butt around the playground, till she passed out.

JOAN: I hope I can stay awake till she goes to bed.

BILL: I'll wake you up. Hey. Everything's not gonna get turned around overnight.

JOAN: I know, I know, I know.

BILL: Like buying new furniture. We'll take our time. We have the rest of our lives, right? What's your hurry?

(BILL kisses JOAN.)

EMILY: *(Offstage)* Let's go Dad, I'm hungry!

BILL: I'm coming, I'm coming, I'm coming!

(BILL exits. We hear EMILY and BILL laughing.)

(Car door slams. Sound of car, on gravel, fading.)

(JOAN *stands still, watching them for a moment.*)

(*Lights shift.* JOAN *addresses the audience.*)

JOAN: Some days, I feel like the Evil Step Mother. I started off as Cinderella's real mother, beloved and sacred, but then she grew up, transforming into a beautiful young woman, and suddenly we all found ourselves playing different parts. When I look in the mirror, my hair has grown tangled and long, my face lined, my fingernails pointy, I feel jealous and mean, I start thinking of poisoned apples. No. I'm not jealous. I just don't want to be the Step Mother.

(*The sound of a gunshot.* JOAN *freezes. A* HUNTER *walks along the edge of the trees without looking at her, then exits.* JOAN *runs to the door of the house, tries again to pick the lock*)

(*Lights shift*)

Scene Two

(*Afternoon. A few days later, inside the house. Boxes are everywhere.* BILL *enters carrying a box, puts it down, opens another box, searching.*)

BILL: How am I supposed to find anything in this disaster? Joan, have you seen my pants?

(BILL *jumps back, hand to his chest as he sees* KAREN *sitting in the corner smoking a cigarette.*)

BILL: *Holy shit*, Karen! Didn't see you sitting there! (*Takes a breath*) Did you see my blue pants?

KAREN: No, sorry, but…nice legs.

BILL: Thought we left you in Pittsburgh.

KAREN: Smuggled myself into one of the boxes.

BILL: Not that I'm not happy to see you. Just not when I'm getting dressed.

KAREN: I'll close my eyes. Thought you'd be working.

BILL: I moved out here to be closer to work, but it doesn't stop me from being late.

KAREN: I have a theory that men have a different sense of time than women.

BILL: I had it timed perfectly, I just didn't think I'd be hunting for clothes to wear—*Joan!*

KAREN: I think women *add* time—for the unexpected... problem.

JOAN: *(Off, stepping on* KAREN's *line)* What!

BILL: Did you see my blue pants?

JOAN: *(Enters)* I found the coffee pot. Now if I can find the coffee.

BILL: A little cooperation wouldn't hurt, especially since I'm gonna be getting my head beat in tonight.

JOAN: Sorry, I didn't know it was my job to keep track of your clothes.

BILL: I'm not asking you to keep track of anything, I'm just asking if you've seen them.

JOAN: No. I haven't. Seen them. I haven't seen a lot of things. I feel like I've lost everything in this move. Try one of the wardrobes in the bedroom.

BILL: I looked already they're not in there.

JOAN: Wear something else.

BILL: I wanted to wear those blue pants.

JOAN: I go through this with Emily every morning.

KAREN: I find, if I lay my clothes out a night, I have a much easier time in the morning.

JOAN: Yeah, but it's not morning, oh my god, it's three o'clock, you're late already, why do you wait till the last minute! They're gonna start docking your pay.

BILL: I need something to wear; I don't need someone yelling at me right now.

JOAN: In my next life I want to be a Buddhist monk. They're only allowed two hundred possessions.

KAREN: I've got five times that in my bathroom alone.

JOAN: There they are.

KAREN: Ooops. Sorry. Didn't see them there when I sat down.

JOAN: *(Hands them to* BILL*)* It's all right, there's shit everywhere. You're welcome.

BILL: Thank you. *(Exits, putting them on)*

KAREN: Maybe you should go easy on him, he's gonna be landing planes in a little while.

JOAN: I'm not gonna be held hostage to his job the rest of my damn life; we walk on eggshells around him as it is.

KAREN: Didn't mean to open up that box.

JOAN: He can get himself dressed without his job coming into it.

*(*BILL *enters, pulling on his coat)*

BILL: I'm gone. G'bye. *(Kisses* JOAN's *cheek)* Going out for a beer after work. Don't wait up. Love you.

JOAN: Love you too.

KAREN: Don't crash any planes! Haha. Just kiddin.

BILL: I'd lose points if I did that. See ya.

(They are quiet for a moment, until BILL *exits.)*

JOAN: Be glad you're single, that's all I can say.

KAREN: Sometimes I am, listening to all my married friends and their problems. Not that you two are having problems.

JOAN: I don't know what we're having. We haven't had sex in about a hundred years.

KAREN: Well, there you go.

JOAN: He's been working a lot of evenings.

KAREN: Wait up one night, a little vino, a little nightgown.

JOAN: *(Considers for a beat, then shifting gears) I hate moving!* I feel like my whole life is teetering on the edge of a huge canyon, when really everything's great. We've got this great house, which took a year to be built and I couldn't wait and now it's done and now we're here and I don't know what the hell I'm going to do out in the country.

KAREN: It's a long way from Queens.

JOAN: I want a sidewalk! So I can walk somewhere and get a cup of coffee.

KAREN: Maybe we can scrounge up a teabag. *(Begins looking in a box)* How's Emily like it out here?

JOAN: She hates it, of course, there's nothing to do, a new school, she's having trouble making friends. Just one more reason to hate her mother. She should be home soon.

KAREN: Well, I miss you already.

JOAN: I didn't expect to feel so isolated. Tell me it's still a day trip. I can meet you for lunch next time.

KAREN: You better.

JOAN: We just thought, the city schools, Emily at this age. The drugs, the everything, I wanted to save her from all that.

KAREN: Drugs are all over.

JOAN: Guns? Gangs? They're not out here.

KAREN: Are you kidding? Every boy over five's got a gun out here.

JOAN: They're called "hunters".

KAREN: Yeah, and all you hear on the local news is the whacko stuff that happens. "Some guy in Westmoreland County chops up his wife and stuffs her in a garbage can."

JOAN: I don't watch the news, and we're not in Westmoreland County.

KAREN: Doesn't matter, it's all depressed except for people like you building beautiful homes, meanwhile your neighbor's a sheep farmer.

JOAN: He is not.

KAREN: I saw some kind of farm animal.

JOAN: It's a goat, or something, it's the kid's pet.

KAREN: Whatever. It was eating grass.

JOAN: Are you trying to make me feel better, Karen?

KAREN: Look, not to make you worried, it's beautiful, really, but driving up that road to your house, reminded me of Unsolved Mysteries.

JOAN: Great.

KAREN: There's something to be said for the city. All those people around, keeping an eye on each other.

JOAN: I'm from New York, remember.

KAREN: Hey, Pittsburgh's a city, even if it's a baby city.

JOAN: Just say, "I told you so", and get it over with.

(Sound of a not too distant gunshot)

KAREN: What the hell was that?

JOAN: I don't know. A hunter? *(Beat)* What am I gonna do out here?

KAREN: *(Referring to a plate of cookies)* Did you bake these?

(JOAN nods, KAREN bites into one)

KAREN: You know what you should do. Buy a horse.

JOAN: Oh, right, we can't buy furniture.

KAREN: You gotta do something for yourself. Take riding lessons. Horses are great. I took lessons somewhere out here when I was a teenager.

JOAN: Actually, there is something I want to do. Don't laugh.

KAREN: What?

JOAN: I want…to write a book.

KAREN: I didn't know you were a writer.

JOAN: I wrote poetry in college. You're laughing! Hey, I majored in English literature.

KAREN: You wanna write, like a novel?

JOAN: For young adults. Well, for girls. I want to write something for Emily, to help her at this age, you know, keep her "power". And that was part of the deal, moving out here. I wouldn't have to work at the bank; I could stay home and try to write. But I haven't had time yet…

KAREN: I think that's great.

JOAN: You do?

KAREN: Yeah, definitely. Girls need real stories, not Cinderella- romantic-love is gonna save you crap. Give em stories that can help them do something. Number one, don't take typing. I wish somebody told me that. That way you'd never end up working as a secretary in a bank having an affair with your married boss. Of

course, there are perks; I'm not washing his socks. His
wife does that. Oops. Sorry. You were saying. You're
writing a book.

JOAN: It's stupid. Everything I think of is stupid. I have
twelve years of children's books in my head, all I can
think of is "Once upon a time…"

KAREN: Forget the books. What were you doing at her
age?

JOAN: Forget it, I don't want to give her any ideas.

KAREN: They'd be cautionary tales, right?

JOAN: I keep thinking about something, but it's too
dark really.

KAREN: Dark I like.

JOAN: No, this is weird.

KAREN: Weird is great. Kids love weird.

JOAN: I want to write a contemporary Rumpelstilskin.

KAREN: Yeah…

JOAN: There's this young girl, eleven or twelve, and
she's in trouble and has a problem or something…

KAREN: Right…

JOAN: And this little dwarf…

KAREN: Little people. You don't call them dwarves
anymore.

JOAN: This weird little guy crawls into her bedroom
window and helps her to solve the problem, right, and
so now she's indebted to him—

KAREN: He crawls into her bedroom window?

JOAN: Will you let me explain it? The point is she has to
name him, right, like in the real story. As soon as she
names him he loses his power and she gains hers.

KAREN: Because…she guesses his name?

JOAN: As soon as I say it out loud, it sounds stupid.

KAREN: Maybe it'll be different on the page. You know how when you tell somebody about a movie, it's not the same thing as seeing it?

JOAN: Just say what you mean: you hate it.

KAREN: What do I know about novel writing?

JOAN: About as much as I do which is nothing. *(Beat)* I should just learn to knit! If I knew how to knit, I could make sweaters. Then, I could teach Emily to knit and she'd have a craft, so she could identify herself by what she could do.

KAREN: Knitting?

JOAN: And not what she looked like! You should see how she's starving herself. I can't stand it.

KAREN: Cause it reminds you of yourself.

JOAN: I don't know what to do with her.

KAREN: Write the book.

JOAN: It's stupid, I'm stupid.

KAREN: Even if it is dumb, it'll keep you outta trouble and away from the farm animals.

(EMILY enters, carrying her book bag, etc)

KAREN: Well, look who's here!

JOAN: Hi. How was school?

EMILY: It was okay. Hi, Karen. You came all the way out to the country to visit us. Good to see you.

KAREN: Hey sweetie. Look at you. I like the outfit. What?

EMILY: Don't comment on how I look. Right, Ma?

JOAN: You're more than what you look like. You've got a brain.

KAREN: Of course, you do, you're brilliant, but I still like the outfit. Give a kiss. You makin friends?

JOAN:You want something to eat?

EMILY: No. They're snots out here. And stupid on top of it.

JOAN: That attitude will make you lots of friends.

EMILY: I have lots of friends. They're just two hours away.

KAREN: I'd be happy to drive somebody out here, when I'm coming. Or you can stay in Pittsburgh some weekend. Anytime.

EMILY: Thanks, Kar, you're the best.

JOAN: I want your room unpacked and everything put away before dinner.

EMILY: You may change your mind after I tell you what happened.

JOAN: What happened?

EMILY: Some girl from school got kidnapped from her bus stop by a psycho killer. She's been missing for three days and they're out searching for her body.

JOAN: (Overlapping) What!?

EMILY: She's like the second girl in six months. Great place you picked to get away from the scary city, wow, I feel safe out here.

JOAN: Wait a minute, what girl?

KAREN: Oh, you know what, I heard about this on the news, I didn't think it was near you.

EMILY: She was waiting at the bus stop her mom said, but she never got on the bus.

JOAN: What happened to the other girl? What makes them think it's a serial killer?

EMILY: I don't know all the details, Mom, all I know is they think it's some maniac, like Son of Sam. Boo.

KAREN: Son of Sam?

JOAN: *(To* EMILY*)* What do you know about Son of Sam?

EMILY: He was some guy who's dog told him to kill people.

KAREN: Oh yeah, yeah, yeah, he was shooting people making out in cars, in the seventies, right?

JOAN: Maybe this girl just ran away.

EMILY: The other one they found "sexually abused and strangled" in the woods, and she disappeared from a bus stop too.

KAREN: Guess you'll be driving her to school.

EMILY: No way. I'm in eighth grade not kindergarten.

JOAN: I'm not going to let you wait at the bus stop by yourself until I know what's going on.

EMILY: Still want me to unpack those boxes?

JOAN: Yes. You're not getting out of that.

EMILY: Then can I call Stephanie? I promised I'd call her after school today.

JOAN: After you unpack and I want everything hanging up in the closet!

EMILY: *(Exiting)* Slave driver.

JOAN: I'm calling the school. They should tell you about this.

KAREN: Don't panic until you find out more about it.

JOAN: If their buses are picking up your kids they're responsible for getting them there safely, aren't they? I'm calling Bill. *(Picks up phone and starts dialing)*

KAREN: He's probably not there yet.

JOAN: I'll call his cell phone.

KAREN: Tell him when he gets home. There are people on those planes.

JOAN: *(Ear to phone, listening)* Emily, get off the phone, I said after you unpack those boxes. Do it now. *(Hangs up)* What am I gonna do with that kid.

KAREN: She's fine.

JOAN: You should be her mother. She likes you better.

KAREN: That's because I'm *not* her mother.

(EMILY suddenly screams offstage)

JOAN: What the hell is going on now!

EMILY: *Mom!* I cut myself! I'm bleeding!

JOAN: What did you do?!

EMILY: I didn't do anything.

JOAN: Let me see. You're bleeding!

EMILY: There's blood all over my bedspread.

JOAN: Em-i-lee! What were you doing?

EMILY: I was trying to open a box with the razor blade and it slipped.

JOAN: How many times do I have to tell you, you gotta pay attention to what you're doing. You're lucky you didn't slice off your finger.

KAREN: Hold the towel and press it.

JOAN: Damn, I don't know where we packed the first aide stuff.

KAREN: I might have some bandaids in my bag.

JOAN: I think it's gonna need more than bandaids.

EMILY: Stitches!? *No!!*

JOAN: If we can't stop the bleeding we'll have to go to the hospital.

KAREN: *(Digging through her purse)* Calm down, Joanie, it's just blood.

JOAN: But it's in a bad spot, look, it's right where she bends her thumb.

EMILY: I don't want stitches!

KAREN: All's you need is the butterfly stitch. Whenever one of us cracked our heads open, which, with the size of my family, was every other day, my mother squeezed, spit, stuck a bandaid on it, we were fine. Here we go. *(Pulls a Kotex out of her purse)* Just wrap it around.

EMILY: You're not putting that on my hand.

KAREN: It's for bleeding, isn't it?

EMILY: Ew, gross!

(The women start laughing as KAREN bandages EMILY:)

KAREN: *(To JOAN)* She's *okay!*

JOAN: *(Kissing EMILY on the forehead)* Be more careful. Please.

KAREN: Crisis averted. Cookie?

(EMILY takes cookie.)

(Lights shift. EMILY and KAREN exit.)

(JOAN addresses the audience.)

JOAN: This is what I want to know: how come we never hear the story about Little Red Riding Hood's Mother? What about her side of it? Standing on the doorstep, watching Little Red as she disappears round the bend into the dark woods. Heart beating, hands wringing, hyperventilating, completely powerless, frozen on that doorstep. What the hell was the matter with her? Letting her defenseless child walk through the woods by herself with a maniac wolf on the loose? She knew full well that forest was full of wolves, but she sent her out there with a basketful of bait! "Stay on the path," like that's gonna save her. It's almost like she wanted little Red out of the way. Maybe she couldn't stand the pressure of living in the woods anymore, the isolation, doing nothing but baking cookies for her sick mother, and you never hear about that relationship, why doesn't she visit her sick mother herself? And where was Little Red's father, no one every addresses that. And what about the Woodcutter? A strange man in the woods with an ax. Why does everyone automatically trust him?

(Sound of an ax falling swiftly, then a loud thud)

(Lights shift.)

Scene Three

(A candle is burning. JOAN *is sitting on the floor with a bottle of wine, two glasses, wrapped in a comforter. Pours herself another glass of wine. Drinks it, then blows out the candle.* BILL *enters and trips over her in the dark.)*

BILL: Whuh—?

JOAN: It's me, it's me, I'm here, I'm sitting here.

BILL: What are you doing sitting on the floor in the dark?

JOAN: I was waiting for you.

BILL: I told you not to wait up.

JOAN: I know, I know, I just thought I would. Dumb idea.

BILL: Why not turn on a light?

JOAN: I was going for a mood.

BILL: Well, you got one: terror.

JOAN: Sorry. You smell like the bar.

BILL: That's where I was. Was this for me?

JOAN: Yeah.

BILL: *(Pours himself a glass)* Thank you. This is nice.

JOAN: I managed to start a fire, but it burned out.

BILL: I told you I was going out.

JOAN: I know. So, how was work?

BILL: Is that a question you want an answer to?

JOAN: Don't do that. I could go to bed.

BILL: I just spent the last three hours talking about work, so I don't have the need to talk, unless you want to.

JOAN: Something happen?

BILL: Something always happens. Low time pilots, traffic managers not doing their jobs, center keeps pumping them, so I keep batting them away, till somebody yells, "Stop departures".

JOAN: I mean, like, an emergency—?

BILL: Or a deal. Or a fight with a supervisor. No, your husband did not fuck up tonight.

JOAN: I'm not saying that. Oh my god, Bill. I'm trying. Isn't that what wives are supposed to say, how was work?

BILL: My trainee is low on hours. We were talking about her.

JOAN: Who?

BILL: I told you about her, this girl, this woman, I'm training.

JOAN: Does she have a name?

BILL: I told you about her, Joan, her name is Lisa.

JOAN: So you went out with Lisa?

BILL: Our crew went out to talk about work. I appreciate your making the effort, but I know you don't really want to hear about it. Let's talk about something else.

JOAN: *(Beat)* You can ask me how it was here.

BILL: *(Beat)* How was it here?

JOAN: Karen stuck around a while, which was a good thing, because Emily cut her hand wide open, opening a box with a razor blade.

BILL: She need stitches?

JOAN: Karen did the old butterfly stitch with a kotex. *(Starts giggling)* We didn't have, well, I couldn't find the bandaids—

BILL: I don't need all the bloody details.

JOAN: She's having a hard time.

BILL: She'll be fine once she makes some friends.

JOAN: Something else happened today. A girl was kidnapped from her bus stop.

BILL: Yeah, I heard about that at work.

JOAN: And you didn't tell me?

BILL: I was going to. Don't overreact.

JOAN: A serial killer is something I should react to.

BILL: It's not the same guy. The one had a whacko boyfriend, the other had problems at home, she probably ran away.

JOAN: But her mother said she saw her standing at the bus stop and the bus driver says she never got on.

BILL: Are we gonna argue about this, cause if we are let's say we did, you won, and now you're not talking to me, because that's where this is heading.

JOAN: I didn't stay up to argue. I thought we were going to try and work on things.

BILL: And that's what we're doing, but its gonna take time, Joan, you can't expect—

JOAN: I miss you.

BILL: Commere.

JOAN: I thought if we moved closer to the airport, we'd have more time. I never see you.

BILL: I'm right here.

JOAN: And all we do is fight.

BILL: *(Kissing her)* We stopped fighting. What?

JOAN: Take off from work, a few days.

BILL: I can't. I'm out of annual.

JOAN: Call in sick.

BILL: I'm low on sick leave.

JOAN: Family leave, then.

BILL: I can't right now, Joan.

JOAN: When you want time off to go someplace with your buddies you move heaven and earth, work out all kinds of convoluted schedules to get off. All I'm asking is for you to do the same for me, for us, for once put your family up there as a priority.

BILL: My family is the priority, which is why I have no annual left. I took a week off to move and now I have to work, because somebody's gotta pay the mortgage.

JOAN: And I quit my job.

BILL: And I think it's a good idea for you to take some time off, settle Emily into the new house, maybe, do some laundry.

JOAN: I didn't quit to become a country housewife.

BILL: You can do whatever you want.

JOAN: I need to spend some time with you. Why is that so threatening?

BILL: I'm not threatened; I'm tapped out.

JOAN: Are you foolin around, cause if you are, Bill, you should just tell me.

BILL: When would I have the time? Time. That's the problem. Look. We want to spend more time together, of course we do, but we just incurred about twice as much debt, so now I have to work, to pay off the debt. We moved! That's stressful! The house is out of control, and you have to take care of that. I will help you. But, what that means is less time. Now shhh. Since we have so little time, we have to make the most of the time we have. You waited up, let's not waste it.

(BILL *takes* JOAN's *arms and gently, seductively, pulls them behind her. He kisses her. She pulls away.*)

JOAN: I can't.

BILL: Yes you can.

JOAN: No. I can't just go from being all upset, to making love. I need to talk some more.

BILL: I love you. Do you love me?

JOAN: I feel like something terrible is going to happen.

BILL: Nothing is gonna happen.

(BILL *presses* JOAN *back. She lets herself be kissed. As they make love, lights start to fade, then* BILL *rolls over and goes to sleep,* JOAN *sits up.*)

JOAN: Can you hear my heart beating? That's what I want to ask him. After we pound our bodies at each other, and I come in a rock hard explosion, "Can you hear it?" But I don't. I get up and walk through the empty rooms to the bathroom. Emily's bedroom door

is open. I go in and call her name. The curtains are
blowing out the window and my heart freezes. Her
bed is empty. Then I remember how she used to hide
under the covers when she was a baby, so I pull off
the comforter. But she isn't there, the sheets are all
bunched up and I feel around for her with my hands
and rip the top sheet off, then the bottom sheet, to the
bare mattress. I run my hands over it, feeling for a
crack that she might've slipped through, until I finally
pull off the mattress and there under the bed is a hole.
A clean, round, deep black hole, leading down. I yell
into the hole: Rumpelstilskin! That's your name, you
bastard, I know your name! But all I hear is my heart
beating. *(Beat)* Then I wake up.

(Lights shift)

Scene Four

(Two weeks later. Morning. JOAN *and* KAREN *are having
coffee, surrounded by the same half unpacked boxes.* JOAN
*is holding a mess of yarn and needles. Sound of gunshot
outside, this time, a little closer.* KAREN *jumps.* JOAN
ignores it.)

JOAN: *(Referring to her knitting)* I thought it would be
therapeutic.

KAREN: Want to talk about it?

JOAN: When he's on evenings he sleeps till noon, I can't
go near him for three hours after he wakes up, then he
goes to work. I try staying up till he comes home, but
he goes out for a beer, and I fall asleep on the couch.
When he's on daylight, he works an hour comp time so
he doesn't get home till after Emily. I cook dinner, by
the time Emily's in bed, I'm ready to pass out. How can
we work on our relationship if we're never awake at
the same time?

KAREN: Have you had sex yet? With each other?

JOAN: Do you think he's having an affair?

KAREN: You mean, in my capacity as "the other woman" do I smell another woman?

JOAN: I didn't mean it like that.

KAREN: You didn't answer my question.

JOAN: Yes, we've had sex!

KAREN: Good. That should relieve some pressure. As far as another woman, Bill doesn't strike me as the type. But then again, I haven't tested the waters. I'm kidding.

JOAN: Gimme my sweater, I just need a hobby.

KAREN: That's a sweater?

JOAN: Maybe I need something a little easier.

KAREN: Want some advice?

JOAN: Don't tell me I should write a book. I'm not a writer. Besides, Rumpelstilskin's been done.

KAREN: I was gonna suggest unpacking.

JOAN: Between the farm animals and the serial killers, I haven't decided if I'm staying.

KAREN: That's a problem.

JOAN: It's too quiet! I need to hear garbage trucks outside my window. Especially at night. It's too dark. Bill said we should get a dog, on his way out the door.

KAREN: Might be a good idea.

JOAN: Of course, he'll want a golden retriever and I'll be the one training it, might's well have another baby. They at least grow up. A dog is like a perpetual two year old.

KAREN: A two year old doesn't bite the burglar in the ass.

JOAN: I don't want a dog! I want to learn how to knit! But I can't learn it from a book! Somebody has to teach you, it has to be passed down. Know anybody who knits?

KAREN: Hey, I looked up your pal on the internet. Guess what? Ol' Son of Sammy has his own webpage!

JOAN: *(Trying to untangle the knotted knitting)* Please don't tell me about it.

KAREN: How old were you when he was—?

JOAN: Fifteen going on sixteen.

KAREN: I would've hid under my bed.

JOAN: We stayed out all night and went to places we thought he'd be. The park, lovers lane, the street in Forest Hills where he actually killed somebody. I don't know what we were looking for.

KAREN: Where was your mother?

JOAN: Told her I was staying at a friend's house and she believed me.

KAREN: I would've locked you in your room.

JOAN: I'm talking to you and it's all I can do to restrain myself from running out that door, driving to the school and barging into her classroom just to make sure she's there.

KAREN: You could call them.

JOAN: I drove her to school this morning and waited outside until I saw her walk into the building with my own eyes. She didn't speak to me the whole way down there. She said if I'm there when she gets out, she'll never speak to me again. She has no fear.

KAREN: Maybe you should write your book about Son of Sam. Moms, want to teach your daughters fear: read them "Tales from the Seventies."

JOAN: I don't want to think about the seventies.

KAREN: No one who lived through them does! All those people doing the retro thing were born in the Eighties or Nineties! Although I do like some of the shoes. Remember spike heels? *(Referring to her own shoes)* That's what they are! *(Stops)* Are you picking her up from school today?

JOAN: Yes. *(Starts to put away her "knitting")* You drive all the way out here to listen to me ramble on about my problems. I never ask about you. How's old what's his name?

KAREN: Still married.

JOAN: Thank him for me, for giving you the morning off.

KAREN: One of the perks you get for messing around with the boss.

JOAN: I don't get any mornings off.

KAREN: Maybe you need to mess around.

JOAN: We did.

KAREN: I meant with somebody else.

JOAN: Yeah, right. With who? There's nobody out here.

KAREN: Maybe the goat boy next door.

JOAN: Or the mailman. Who I have never seen. Besides, I don't think it would improve Bill's mood.

KAREN: No, but it might help yours.

JOAN: Or it might give him the excuse to finally kill me.

KAREN: Don't worry about Bill. What's his name is the same way this time of year. It's the season. It will pass.

JOAN: Football season?

KAREN: Deer season. But it's no accident it coincides with football season. I have a theory: something in their blood makes them more aggressive during deer season.

JOAN: Bill doesn't hunt.

KAREN: Doesn't matter. Somebody should do a survey to find out the percentage of domestic abuse from October to January. I bet it goes up.

JOAN: Don't be telling me this, I got deer hiding from hunters behind my house.

KAREN: Look at a deer. Can you think of a more feminine animal that men so gleefully hunt down and kill? There's a whole ritual to it, the clothes, the equipment, the way they stake them out, all to murder a basically defenseless animal. Who killed Bambi's mother? I mean something instinctual is going on here, whether they're controlling deer population or airplanes. Then it spills over, when they're dealing with you. My advice: till deer season is over: lay low.

(JOAN *thinks about this for a beat, then*)

JOAN: I remember Stacy Moskowitz because she was the last person he killed. It was nearing the one year anniversary and everybody was saying they were gonna catch him, when *bang*. They had her picture in the paper, like a before and after. In one, she's smiling, curly blond hair pushed back from her face, one of those girls everybody wants to be, and in the other she's on a stretcher, her face all purple and swollen. I saw her mother on a talk show about ten years later, and she had these earrings down to her shoulders, the woman had the longest earlobes I'd ever seen. I remember thinking, those earrings are like her sadness, pulling her down.

(*Both are silent.* EMILY *enters smiling brightly*)

JOAN: What are you doing home?

EMILY: Half day.

JOAN: They don't tell the parents?

EMILY: It's a Teacher In-Service day. It was in the calendar.

JOAN: But how did you get home?

EMILY: Bus.

JOAN: I can't believe this. I'm callin the school.

EMILY: Mom. It's okay, I'm home. Hi Kar.

(EMILY *kisses* KAREN.)

KAREN: How's my girl? Sharp outfit. How are your grades?

EMILY: Straight A's. Cool shoes.

KAREN: Thanks.

EMILY: *(Kisses* JOAN*)* And how was your morning?

JOAN: *(Smiling)* My morning was okay. What's going on, Emily?

EMILY: I had a good morning, just asking how yours was.

JOAN: My morning was fine. I didn't learn how to knit.

EMILY: Mom, when are you going to judge yourself not by what you can do, but by who you *are*.

KAREN: Out of the mouths of babes.

JOAN: You want a smack? I mean snack?

EMILY: Sure.

JOAN: Oh, now I'm really suspicious.

EMILY: What? I'm hungry. It's lunchtime. *(Opening a box of dishes, unpacking)*

JOAN: What are you doing?

EMILY: I'm helping you.

JOAN: Okay, what do you want, I know you want something.

EMILY: If you say yes, I'll help you unpack all the rest of the boxes and I won't quit until it's done. I got invited to go to a sleepover at this girl Marilyn's. There's about five other girls going and they invited me!

JOAN: When?

EMILY: Next Friday—it's *not* a Halloween party, just a sleepover.

JOAN: And where is it?

EMILY: Marilyn's Dad's…cabin.

JOAN: What do you mean, cabin?

EMILY: Her Dad has a cabin. Not far.

JOAN: In the woods? What are they divorced, "her Dad's cabin."

EMILY: What does that matter?

JOAN: Will one of her parents be there?

EMILY: Her older sister will be there.

JOAN: How much older.

EMILY: She's sixteen. But, she's gonna be seventeen!

JOAN: And where is it, in the woods? Does it have electricity? A phone?

EMILY: I don't know; it's on her parents' land up past the school! And yes, it's in the woods, everything's in the woods around here.

JOAN: I don't think so.

EMILY: I can bring your cell phone!

JOAN: No.

EMILY: You want me to make friends and then when I finally do, you tell me I can't go!

JOAN: I'm not telling you, you can't make friends, I'm telling you I don't want you in the middle of the woods at night without adult supervision—

EMILY: But her sister's gonna be there!

JOAN: —with a serial killer on the loose!

EMILY: Ugh. I knew it. It's *not* a serial killer. They were totally unrelated murders.

JOAN: Two weeks ago you told me it was a serial killer.

EMILY: Well, now they've decided it isn't.

JOAN: Two girls have still been killed.

EMILY: If you stopped your life every time some girl got murdered.

KAREN: Maybe you should.

EMILY: Your life would be at a standstill! Somebody is always out there murdering people. This is not about dead girls, this is about her being afraid.

JOAN: I'm not afraid.

EMILY: First you're afraid of the city; then you're afraid of the country—

JOAN: I'm not having this conversation. Go to your room and start your homework.

EMILY: She's afraid of the harmful effects of television, she's afraid of hormones in the milk and genetically altered potatoes. She can't put something in her mouth without washing it a hundred times because she's afraid of pesticides, but she's also afraid of the water: city water, well water, ground water. Doesn't matter she's afraid of it.

JOAN: That's enough.

EMILY: No, because you're also afraid of me making friends, because then I won't need you anymore, because what you're really afraid of is me growing up.

You're afraid then you'll have to deal with *your own
life*! This is your fear, Mom and it's strangling me!

JOAN: *(Overlapping on fear)* You are not grown up, you
are thirteen years old and I think you better take a time
out before you say another word.

EMILY: Fine. But I know why we moved up here! So
you can keep me in *prison*! *(She storms off.)*

KAREN: It's all right. It's over. You did a good job.
You're a good mother. She's blessed to have you.

EMILY: *(Offstage)* And don't bother making me dinner!
I'll just eat *bread and water*!

KAREN: Even if she doesn't know it yet.

JOAN: She's the only person who can do this to me. I'm
afraid if I let any of it out on her, I'd *kill her. I would just
kill her.* So, I stuff it down inside, and it's making me
sick. I can't let her go to a sleepover in the woods; she's
thirteen years old!

KAREN: She's too young.

JOAN: I can't worry about her liking me; I have to
protect her.

KAREN: Of course you do.

JOAN: Everybody else moves to the suburbs, why
couldn't we?

KAREN: You moved here because you built the house
that you and Bill have been dreaming of since before
she was born. It doesn't have anything to do with
her; that's why she's mad. And it's a beautiful house.
Gorgeous.

JOAN: Still doesn't have any furniture.

KAREN: No satisfying this woman.

JOAN: I want to go back to our little house in Pittsburgh. I want neighbors breathing down my neck again.

KAREN: You just gotta get used to it. Hey, I gotta get used to you not being there, too. Used to be I could walk over whenever I got a little lonely. Now I gotta plan those lonely attacks in advance.

JOAN: Are you lonely? Karen.

KAREN: Nah. Maybe sometimes. Although when I go home from a good session here, I think, "solitude, I love my solitude." The clock is tickin. But I've been trying to think of myself, not as childless, but as child*free*. I guess there's a price no matter what we choose.

JOAN: Only you don't find out how much till after you've brought it home.

KAREN: Now there's something to put in your book. The price of things: Love: Thirty years. Marriage:

JOAN: Your sanity.

KAREN: Children?

JOAN: Peace of mind. Never again.

(Lights shift. KAREN exits.)

JOAN: *(Striking a match and lighting a candle)* ...baked in ovens, poisoned by witches, eaten by trolls. All the bad things that happen to children in stories. Are they warnings...or wishes...

(Lights shift)

Scene Five

(Later that night. JOAN *is trying to write. She stares at the blank screen.* EMILY *enters.)*

EMILY: Mom?

JOAN: Yeah.

EMILY: Can I talk to you?

JOAN: Yes, you can. Want some tea?

EMILY: No thanks. When's Dad coming home?

JOAN: I don't know, honey, I guess he went out after work.

EMILY: I'm sorry about this afternoon.

JOAN: Me too.

EMILY: It's the first time I've been invited anywhere and I really want to go. I want some friends, Mom.

JOAN: I know you do, Emily, and you'll make friends. Before you ask me again, I want you to listen: I don't have a relationship with my mother.

EMILY: Yes, you do.

JOAN: I couldn't talk to her and I didn't listen to her. I went behind her back and was into all kinds of trouble, and as much as I told myself that I didn't need a mother, I actually needed her very much.

EMILY: Mom, I know I need you.

JOAN: I don't want you to feel about me, the way I felt about my mother: that I couldn't trust her with the truth of my life.

EMILY: I'm not lying. Marilyn's sister is gonna be there.

JOAN: I'm not worried about Marilyn's sister.

EMILY: You can call her father.

JOAN: It's dangerous out there. I hate having to tell you that, because I don't want to make you afraid, but I need to keep you safe.

EMILY: That's what they do out in the country though, they're not afraid of the woods. Their parents trust them.

JOAN: I don't think you're going to do anything bad.

EMILY: I bet Dad says yes.

JOAN: Don't do that. Don't pit us against each other.

EMILY: This is important to me, Mom!

JOAN: There'll be other parties.

EMILY: But if I don't go to this one, I won't be invited to any other parties!

JOAN: I'm sorry. Emily. I cannot let you go out into the woods right now. Do you want me to go against my instincts?

(EMILY *thrusts her hand over the candle flame*)

JOAN: *(Pulling her hand away)* What are you doing? Emily, you're gonna burn yourself. Emily!

EMILY: *(Continuing to put her hand over the flame)*

Don't stop me! See, you keep stopping me! You can't stop me forever!!

JOAN: *(Blows out candle)* I'm not gonna sit here and watch you burn your hand!

EMILY: I'm going to grow up knowing *nothing* about the world!

JOAN: You have an imagination. You don't have to experience the world to know it's dangerous.

EMILY: That's just it, I *want* to experience it!

JOAN: I'm not getting into an argument I can't win.

EMILY: All I get to experience is on television and you hate television.

JOAN: For now you can read books.

EMILY: You're always telling me, "Life is not a fairytale!"

JOAN: That's right, it's not.

EMILY: But the way you're bringing me up, I'm gonna be a scared little rabbit! Please, Mom, I wanna go.

JOAN: No. I have to say no.

EMILY: You can't really protect me. You just think you can. Anything can happen. You're not watching over me every single minute. All your worrying and trying to protect me is good for nothing, because I could still wind up—

JOAN: Don't say another word!

(EMILY *pulls away from* JOAN *and exits.*)

(*Lights shift.*)

JOAN: (*Quickly painting the picture*) Once upon a time, there is a full moon rising over Manhattan. Skyscrapers rise up against it like black teeth ready to bite. Something is paused at the edge of the city, like a rubber band stretched back ready to snap. Then something triggers it, the pull of the moon and it moves, slowly at first, until taillights snake bloody streaks over bridge and tunnel towards Queens. There is no traffic at this hour in the Midtown tunnel, so it flies unheeded along the Long Island expressway between warehouse and highrise, bleeding onto Woodhaven Boulevard, past dark windows, and sleeping storefronts, past trees guarding blind alleys, where broken glass shines like stars. The Jamaica Avenue el train clacks overhead, then a quiet side street. A car door slams, softly, the sound of walking.

(A dark figure appears at the edge of the stage, a presence or memory, as JOAN *continues)*

JOAN: A soft breeze is blowing my mother's curtains over me where I lay breathing in the new leaves of the old tree which follow me in dreaming of the boy who will break my heart that summer. We are making out in Forest Park in the front seat of his brother's car and I am starving for something, to eat or be eaten. I've written my name in the condensation, my finger squeaking on the window. I can see something outside in the trees, a dark something waiting. I am kissed and it moves towards me. He, the boy, is touching me, and I am trying to bury myself in his chest but it's no good, it's out there waiting and when I look up, I meet its face right through the letters of my name.

(As lights fade, EMILY *screams.)*

EMILY: *Mom!!*

(Black out)

Scene Six

(Afternoon. JOAN *enters as* BILL *looks through his mail.)*

JOAN: She's still asleep.

BILL: I don't want to know about this.

JOAN: You don't have to talk to her about it, but you have to know about it.

BILL: This is your area. If we had a boy, then I would deal with that stuff.

JOAN: If we had a boy there would be nothing to deal with.

BILL: Boy's go through changes too.

JOAN: She screamed, and at first I thought she cut herself again, but when I went in there, she was a mess, she seemed to have no idea what was happening to her.

BILL: Didn't you ever tell her what was gonna happen when she got older.

JOAN: I did—that's why I don't understand her reaction.

BILL: Just make sure you talk to her about boys.

JOAN: She's not interested in boys. That's what I mean, she's so young.

BILL: Don't be too sure about that.

JOAN: I'll talk to her. If you talk to her about that party in the woods.

BILL: She's had sleepovers before.

JOAN: Not in the woods.

BILL: They're gonna be inside, not outside and there will be a lot of girls, she'll be fine.

JOAN: I don't think you're taking the danger seriously.

BILL: What danger?

JOAN: There is somebody in this area, county, whatever you call this place we're in, this "dark part of the forest" —it's certainly not a neighborhood—

BILL: It's a community.

JOAN: Whatever. There's something out there. Until they catch it, I'm taking precautions to protect our daughter and I can't believe you aren't.

BILL: There's nothing specific to protect her from, besides the normal dangers, and you can't paralyze your life—

JOAN: Even if the police aren't saying it's the same guy, it's a little strange, don't you think, two girls from the same community disappear in six months. This didn't happen in the city.

BILL: Worse things happen in the city.

JOAN: What were we running away from?

BILL: It was your idea.

JOAN: My idea was private school.

BILL: You said you wanted to protect her from what she'd be exposed to in the city schools. In my book, that extends to the city.

JOAN: It doesn't matter we're stuck here now.

BILL: I work my tail off for a year and a half to afford to build this place, for you, and now you feel stuck.

JOAN: I need to feel safe. Do you feel safe?

BILL: You're blowing this out of proportion.

JOAN: I'm seeing a pattern even if no one else is. I don't want to wait till Emily gets kidnapped for you to believe me.

BILL: *Don't say that!* Listen to me: it's random.

JOAN: Where were you today?

BILL: What do you mean, where was I?

JOAN: I called work; you weren't there.

BILL: I took comp time.

JOAN: Now see, I thought taking comp time meant you were working comp time.

BILL: And sometimes I take a few hours to recover so I don't bring my work shit back home, which you already told me, you can't handle. I can't win with you, I'm doing what you want and I'm still in trouble. A girl wanders off and so I must be to blame.

JOAN: Two girls.

BILL: What are you getting at Joanie. Just say it.

JOAN: I don't want Emily going to that party.

BILL: Didn't you go to parties as a kid?

JOAN: When I was a teenager in New York, Son of Sam was killing young girls. It feels the same way to me.

BILL: It's not even remotely the same.

JOAN: Women. It's about killing women.

BILL: He didn't kill any men?

JOAN: Yes, he did, but the targets were women. And it's starting again. Only this time they're younger—and I have this sense of, of becoming *prey*.

BILL: I don't know what you're talking about.

JOAN: Bill, something happened to me then, and it feels like it's coming back now, triggered by these murders and I don't know what to do with it.

BILL: Are you telling me you were raped or something?

JOAN: Why, would that turn you on?

BILL: No, it would not turn me on.

JOAN: I'm just asking because lately it seems like something that would interest you.

BILL: I'm confused now. Are we talking about Emily, the missing girls, Son of Sam, your rapist husband? Just what are we talking about?

JOAN: Our sex life.

BILL: Give me a minute to make that turn.

JOAN: I don't like the way it's been lately.

BILL: It hasn't been lately.

JOAN: It's not the roughness, really—or the — it's more the way you hold my wrists. The way you put my arms back—

BILL: I only started doing that because you liked it.

JOAN: I don't like it anymore.

BILL: I'll stop doing it.

JOAN: It doesn't feel like love.

BILL: You never touch me. You make me beg for it every time. That doesn't feel like love either.

JOAN: I can't talk to you.

BILL: I think you better talk to somebody.

JOAN: So, now I'm crazy.

BILL: I didn't say that.

JOAN: Because I'm afraid of my daughter being killed, when girls are being killed? Because I'm wondering where my husband is when he says he's working when he's not? Because I don't like it when you hurt me when we're having sex!? *I should talk to you, that's who I should talk to.*

BILL: I am not the enemy. *(Pause)* I'm your husband and I used to be your friend.

JOAN: My friends don't make me feel like this.

BILL: Don't they? I like Karen, don't get me wrong, but you're always more unhappy after you talk to her.

JOAN: Maybe that's because with her I talk about what's going on, instead of pretending it's not happening.

(EMILY *enters quietly, looks at* JOAN, *then to* BILL.)

EMILY: She was watching me today. I saw her from the school yard sitting in her car spying on me!

JOAN: Honey, I wasn't spying on you. I got there early to pick you up, so I was just waiting.

EMILY: Two hours early! Daddy, she's breathing down my neck every single second! I can't take it anymore.

JOAN: *(To BILL)* We'll talk about it later.

EMILY: She won't let me go to the party! I have to tell them today.

BILL: I got no problem with it.

JOAN: Well, I do.

EMILY: See??

JOAN: This is something we should discuss between us later.

BILL: Fine. You wanna discuss, we'll discuss, which means you talk and I'll listen until I agree with you.

JOAN: That isn't fair.

EMILY: You're talking about me as if I'm not here.

JOAN: That's because you brought this up and it's something your father and I have to agree on first.

EMILY: But he agrees with me!

BILL: *(Beat)* You heard your mother.

(EMILY exits, infuriated.)

BILL: Ease up on her, or you're gonna drive her away. I'm not threatening you, so don't think I am, I'm trying, God knows I am, but the same thing goes for me.

(BILL exits. Lights shift.)

JOAN: The irony, of course, is that they did everything they could. All sharp, shiny, potential weapons from steak knives to box cutters to hat pins were banished from the entire kingdom. But she pricked her finger anyway. *(Beat)* And when the dark unforgiving bubble of blood burst through the tender skin of her pinky finger, a silent accusation bloomed within it, full of the secret of how deep it went, her life's blood welling on the head of the pin—until blotting out the sun, it put them all to sleep, for one hundred years.

(The phone rings and rings, stopping in the middle of the third ring. Lights shift. BILL *appears in the green glow of radar screens. He wears a headset and is talking to airplanes when he answers* JOAN's *call.)*

JOAN: Bill—

BILL: ...Yeah.

JOAN: Are you on position?

BILL: Go ahead. I can talk.

JOAN: She got on the bus. I walked her to the bus stop. Kissed her good bye and saw her get on the bus.

BILL: Hold on... *(Into headset)* U S Air Seven, Traffic Ten-thirty, seven miles southbound descending to six thousand a Boeing Seven Fifty-seven.

JOAN: The school called and said she was in her morning class, but she's not there now.

BILL: Maybe she went to a friend's house. Don't panic.

JOAN: Why would she leave school in the middle of the day? Where would she go?

BILL: Isn't that party today?

JOAN: I told her she couldn't go.

BILL: I said she could.

JOAN: I thought we were going to talk about it—

BILL: Hang on...U S Air Seven Say Altitude—I'll call you when I get off position. Meantime, call the parents.

JOAN: I did, I called everybody! Nobody knows where she is!!

BILL: U S Air Seven Descend immediately to five thousand, six thousand traffic twelve o'clock less than a mile. Christ this idiot busted his altitude. *(Without pause, segues into air traffic control phraseology)* U SAir five four niner Roger Reduce speed to two-one zero, then descend and maintain four thousand. Continental Five fifteen immediate right turn, lean into it, captain, traffic on your left, approaching less than a mile— *(To* JOAN*)* I gotta go.

*(*BILL *hangs up. The sounds of pilots and air traffic controllers cuts off suddenly)*

JOAN: Bill! Bill!!

(Lights shift)

*(*STACEY MOSKOWITZ *steps out of the Forest. One side of her face is bruised purple, part of her head blown away. She walks to the swing, speaking to the audience.* JOAN *listens.)*

STACEY: He parked in front of this little playground. I didn't want to do it right there in the car, so I jumped out and ran into the baby park. He started foolin around, climbin on the monkey bars, actin crazy like he was some kind of caveman chasin me. Then we started goin on the swing. He wanted me to sit on his lap and I did. I could feel him under me. We swang for a while. He tried getting up my shirt and I said no, not here, what if some little kid saw us, but of course, that wasn't gonna happen cause it was after midnight, but I din't have to be home till one cuz my mother thought we went to see *The Exorcist. (Beat)* I heard a car door slam. We were kissin and stuff and not payin attention. Then he was like, let's go back in the car, so we went back to the car and started making out when I heard this tappin on the glass, like tap, tap. I looked out my side of the window and there was this guy standing there, and I thought what does he want, he looked like Joe Schmoe, with this stupid smile, like he was gonna

ask me directions. When the windshield shattered into
a million pieces. The sound came after, like a boom
of thunder a mile away. And the glass rained down,
catchin the street light like a storm of diamonds. It was
beautiful. *(She swings a moment, looking at* JOAN.*)*

(Fade to black, the sound of thunder)

Scene Seven

*(*JOAN *sits in front of the door, framed in the black shadows
of large thorns. She's furiously knitting a misshapen blanket,
next to her is a heap of other misshapen, one-armed sweaters,
crooked scarves, insane socks. She is talking before looking
up from her knitting)*

JOAN: A nuclear bomb dropped out of the sky, and
left a decimated, smoking wasteland. No more Henny
Penny, now I am Nagasaki asking, "why?" Like a
shadow play, people behind a screen hold me down,
put me to sleep, then wake me up. Their faces zoom
in and out, their mouths move, but I can't tell what
they're saying. Days, weeks, pass, until they leave
and then, silence. Except for a hard sound behind the
door, like someone strangling. And a roaring in my
ears, which is the sound your life makes when it all
comes crashing down. *(Stops knitting for half a beat, then
continues)* On the twenty-eighth day, I pick up a ball of
yarn the color of a placenta and start knitting. I know
how. My fingers fly, knit one pearl two, I don't know
what they are doing, but they are doing what they
know, have always known, and my mind is finally,
blessedly still. I don't think, I knit. I'm knitting things
she'll need when she comes back, sweaters and socks
and blankets and things. But I'm also knitting a web, to
catch her with, when she comes falling back to me.

(Lights shift. JOAN is still knitting. BILL enters dressed for work. He watches her knit, she ignores him.)

BILL: Joan? Joan. *(Pause)* Do you need anything?

(JOAN stops knitting. Looks at him, briefly, then returns to her knitting. BILL kneels down next to her. Puts a hand on the knitting to stop her. JOAN gently but deliberately pulls her hands away, continues knitting)

BILL: Stop a second. Just for a second. Commere.

(BILL also gently, but deliberately pulls the knitting out of JOAN's hands, puts it down, she looks at it there. He puts his arms around her, to hold her, she doesn't move. She tries to stay in the embrace, but then pulls away, and reaches for the knitting. He sighs, gets up.)

BILL: You see my keys?

JOAN: Where are you going?

BILL: I'm going to work.

(JOAN, who has been sitting on his coat, pulls it out from under her and puts it on.)

BILL: Can I have my coat, please?

JOAN: I don't believe you're going to work.

BILL: I have to, Joan.

JOAN: No, I mean, yes, I can't understand how you *could* go back to work, but no, I don't believe that's where you're going.

BILL: Where else would I go?

JOAN: How can you bear it?

BILL: I can't bear it. That's why I'm going back to work.

JOAN: You're lying to me.

BILL: You're going to believe what you want no matter what I say, so imagine I said it and you still don't believe me.

JOAN: That makes it easy for you, doesn't it? To do what you want.

BILL: Maybe you should think about going back to work.

JOAN: No.

BILL: You need something to do, while we're waiting—

JOAN: *(Cutting him off)* I have my knitting.

BILL: *(Checking his pockets)* I see that. Do you have my keys?

JOAN: You have so many keys. I never realized. I don't know what doors they all open. What secrets lie between us.

BILL: I'm an open book.

JOAN: Like Bluebeard.

(BILL reaches for his coat pocket, but JOAN backs away.)

JOAN: You can't go.

BILL: I don't understand. You don't want to have anything to do with me, until I'm about to leave.

JOAN: I don't want to be alone.

BILL: Neither do I. That's why I'm going.

JOAN: Please.

BILL: What do you want me to do? I can't sit here like some kind of witch trying to conjure her—

JOAN: *Shhh*—don't say it.

BILL: I'm not saying anything, except, I can't sit around like this. I've got to do something.

JOAN: *(Quietly)* I blame you. Just so you know. I blame you for everything. And I'll never forgive you. As long as I live.

BILL: That's ironic, because I blame you. You were driving her away with your overprotective, overbearing, suspicious, jealous attitude.

JOAN: She did *not* run away.

BILL: I believe she did.

JOAN: You do. Well, what if she didn't? What if she's somewhere close and she needs our help, but we think she ran away so we don't look in the most obvious places.

BILL: We have looked everywhere.

JOAN: I know we have. But I can't go back to work. That says, we're done, we give up, we're going back to the normal godforsaken routines of life—without her.

BILL: I'm not saying that—

JOAN: Well I can't do that.

BILL: What are you doing? You're sitting here knitting. What does that say?

JOAN: I'm waiting. For the answer. Maybe while my hands are busy, the answer will come to me.

BILL: That's why I'm going to work. The same reason.

(A momentary truce. BILL tries to touch JOAN again, she pulls way. He pulls back, rejected again.)

JOAN: *(Quietly)* We were afraid. Afraid of all the brown people moving into the neighborhood. It's so typically suburban and boring. Afraid she'd find a black boyfriend. That's why we came out here.

BILL: You are so wrong.

JOAN: Then why'd we move here?

BILL: I was trying to make you happy.

(JOAN begins to laugh, a little uncontrollably)

JOAN: Of course, it's my fault.

BILL: I can't keep doing this.

JOAN: I keep thinking about this movie. A movie I saw when I was her age about this girl who's kidnapped and put in a coffin and buried alive, I think that's what it was called, Buried Alive.

BILL: Stop right there.

JOAN: I try not to, but the pictures squeeze their way into my head. I see her in the dark. There was a little water thing, she could drink from, and some food for a short time, if she rationed it, and the lid to the coffin—

BILL: Don't tell me this.

JOAN: *(Her hand in front of her face)* —was right here. I see her fighting it, the way she would, trying to get out, fingernails scratching, knees banging, bumping her head. I can hear her panicked breathing and the sudden silence as she realizes where she is. Then screaming like she used to in the middle of the night when she had a bad dream—

BILL: *(Suddenly shaking her to shut her up)* Don't you ever get tired of doing this?

JOAN: *(After he stops)* Yes.

BILL: *(Embracing her)* You have no mercy, for me, for yourself, no one.

JOAN: *(Holding onto him)* Why did we push fate? Why couldn't we be happy with what we had? Why would anyone want to hurt a little girl!!

(JOAN suddenly pulls away from BILL. Pause. JOAN pulls the keys out of the coat pocket, hands them to BILL)

BILL: Thank you. Now the coat, please.

JOAN: No.

BILL: Fine. *(He starts to exit.)*

JOAN: I want a divorce.

(Silence)

BILL: If that's what you want. *(He exits.)*

(Several moments pass. Out of the other coat pocket, JOAN *pulls out a pair of women's underwear. Sound of gunshot)*

(Lights shift.)

JOAN: Think about nineteen-seventy-seven. I am sixteen years old with shoulder length brown hair, living on the edge of Brooklyn and Queens, the center of my universe bound together by avenues and boulevards: Jamaica, Atlantic, Woodhaven, Liberty, Pitkin, Conduit. *(Going back to that time)* Vietnam is history, but the copper P O W bracelet is turning my wrist green, to prove it wasn't a dream. Nixon is no longer president and I haven't the vaguest notion of what that means. Except I feel certain that the world is bearing out my suspicions: "Life sucks and then you die."

*(*EMILY *appears as* YOUNG JOAN *in* JOAN's *imagination. As if her presence conjures him,* THE BOY *emerges next, moving towards* YOUNG JOAN *through the following)*

JOAN: The days are getting longer but the nights are just as dark. I'm in love with a boy who wants to fuck me, although I don't admit to myself I'm afraid to go that far.

*(*YOUNG JOAN *reaches the figure, they start to fool around, physically, like teenagers do, until,* THE BOY *pulls her to him.)*

JOAN: Fear is a pill, I take, then forget. Hanging out in the schoolyard with him and his friends, drinkin Colt 45 and chewing carefree bubble gum, till I have to go home. Then I get him to walk me under the el, where he presses me hard against a parked car. I let him reach up under my shirt, dreaming of tongue kissing him forever.

(THE BOY *gradually pushes* YOUNG JOAN *to her knees*)

JOAN: I hold my breath, as he fumbles for my heart in the darkness, blissfully unaware that I am standing downwind of something bad coming to get me. *(She also gets down onto her knees.)* When I open my mouth to breathe, I swallow long desired unexpected love.

(A loud cracking sound, like a gunshot. A door slamming. Lights shift abruptly. THE BOY *is gone,* JOAN *is still clutching the underwear. Lights shift)*

Scene Eight

*(*JOAN *is outside.* KAREN *enters, then discovers* JOAN *sitting on the ground.)*

KAREN: What'cha doing?

JOAN: Standing guard.

KAREN: You don't answer the phone anymore?

JOAN: I don't want to talk to my mother. She calls to ask if we've heard anything, if we're doing everything, if they're searching the woods, if we've called all her friends, if we put her face on a milk carton yet and by the end of the conversation she starts to cry, and I have to comfort her.

KAREN: Who comforts you?

JOAN: I hang up with my mother, then Bill's mother calls and I feel like stabbing myself.

KAREN: Where is Bill?

JOAN: Work.

KAREN: What can I do? Make the beds? Do the dishes? I could go shopping, get some food. Joan?

JOAN: Kar, do you think our thoughts have power, to make things happen? You know, those half realized dreams that fly by, like what if something happened to Emily and Bill and I was finally free...

KAREN: Everyone thinks those thoughts sometimes.

JOAN: I thought I was trying to protect her, but maybe she was right, I didn't want her to have her own life.

KAREN: Do you want to go for a walk?

JOAN: *(Suddenly snapping) No*, I don't want to go for a walk!

JOAN: *(Quieter)* We'll pretend to be walking but I'll be a bloodhound sniffing every tree for a trace of her. I'd rather just sit here...for now.

KAREN: Whatever you need to do.

JOAN: Now that's just it, I don't *know* what I need to do! I think I should, I should *do*. But I don't know how to take action. I only know how to react. Something happens, I have an emotional reaction, then I stop for a while, until the next thing that happens. That could just about sum up my life. What do you think I should do?

KAREN: To start with, I think you should get up off the ground.

JOAN: When I was a teenager and there were serial killers out there, we went *out*, we went *looking*, we made *plans*, we didn't wallow in our fear, we tried to *slay* the dragon. And as insane and as dangerous as that was, it felt right. We felt strong, invincible, powerful. What assholes we were.

KAREN: You want to go looking for him? I'll go with you. We'll hunt down the motherfucker and kill him, if you want.

(JOAN *offers* KAREN *the underwear.*)

KAREN: What is that?

JOAN: They were in Bill's coat pocket.

KAREN: Whose are they?

JOAN: You tell me.

KAREN: How should I know?

JOAN: Too small to be mine. They look about Emily's size, but there's no tag.

KAREN: There's another explanation.

(JOAN *balls up the underwear, back in her pocket*)

JOAN: It would explain why he didn't care. When I said, "*There's a serial killer out here.*" He said, "Welcome to your dream house."

KAREN: Let me see them.

(JOAN *hands* KAREN *the underwear, who takes them by her fingertips.*)

KAREN: These belong to a woman. A small woman. Believe it or not there are women out there with smaller hips than us. I know that's not a happy thought, but it's not as black as where you're going.

JOAN: You have smaller hips than I do.

KAREN: That's not even funny.

JOAN: How do I know?

KAREN: Because I wouldn't do that.

(JOAN *waits for an answer,* KAREN *is silent.* JOAN *takes back the underwear, putting them in her pocket*)

KAREN: Joan. You've got to do something. Talk to people, her friends at school, her friends in Pittsburgh. She was pretty upset, maybe she did run away!

JOAN: *She didn't run away!* Everybody keeps saying that, I know Emily wouldn't do that.

KAREN: Trace her steps again, talk to all the neighbors, including the goat farmers!

JOAN: We already did that!

KAREN: Do it again and again and keep doing it, until you find out something. That's what I would do if she were my daughter.

JOAN: This would've never happened if she were your daughter.

KAREN: I'll do it for you then, okay, I will talk to everybody. If you promise me you'll do something for yourself.

JOAN: Can you please stop being the caretaker for five minutes and leave me the fuck alone.

KAREN: *(Pause)* I'm sorry. I loved—love—Emily. And I love you, Joan. And I hate to see you doing this to yourself.

JOAN: Do you? You don't feel just a little bit vindicated? The woman who had it all, but just couldn't be satisfied, finally lost everything she never appreciated.

KAREN: We're friends, Joan.

JOAN: I don't trust anybody.

(Lights shift. KAREN exits.)

JOAN: What did Gretel do? She left a trail of breadcrumbs. But the birds ate them. What did Snow White do? She swept the floors and made the beds for seven little people. Okay. …What did Medea do?

(Lights shift.)

Scene Nine

(Lights rise as JOAN *raises a knitting needle over her head, then stabs open a box. She pulls out one of* BILL*'s shirts. She runs her hands along it for a moment, smells it, then slowly stabs the knitting needle through it, pulling it down in a long tear.* BILL *enters and grabs her from behind)*

BILL: You can go crazy and knit yourself into a looney bin, but don't you dare threaten me in my own house.

*(*JOAN *pulls away from him, leaving the shredded shirt in his hands)*

JOAN: I'm not threatening you.

BILL: This is not a love letter.

JOAN: It's a metaphor.

BILL: I don't need one of your goddamn metaphors on a sixty- dollar shirt!

*(*BILL *throws the shirt at* JOAN.*)*

JOAN: Why are you wearing sixty-dollar shirts to work? You sit in front of a screen talking to planes in the dark. You used to go to work in tee shirts.

BILL: Why are you always looking for something sinister? Maybe you can try believing, for once, it's something innocent; instead of always searching for ways to make Bill look bad.

JOAN: Maybe I already found what I'm looking for.

BILL: Don't give me that cryptic shit.

JOAN: Maybe you snapped, Bill. Maybe the pressure of everything, it's understandable.

BILL: I'm not the crazy one in this house.

JOAN: At least I'm telling the truth!

BILL: First, I'm a rapist, then I'm a liar, now I'm a nutjob. What're you gonna accuse me of next?

JOAN: Where do you go when you leave here?

BILL: I go to work.

JOAN: Every cell in my body is telling me that isn't true.

(Sound of an airplane coming in on final approach)

BILL: I'm not gonna stand here being accused of I don't even know what—fill in the blank. *(Takes off his shirt, grabbing another one from the box)* I'm going to work.

JOAN: *(She grabs shirt from him and starts ripping it with the knitting needle.)* No, you're not.

BILL: God help me, Joanie, I get my hands on you, I'll kill you.

(BILL lunges for JOAN, but the box blocks his path. She stabs the shirt as many times as she can, then throws it at him, but he grabs her around the waist, pinning her to the floor)

JOAN: I hate you. I can't believe how much I hate you. How could I have ever loved you?

BILL: Then why the hell did you marry me?

JOAN: Because I trusted you not to hurt me. Because I thought you were safe, goddamn you, and now I don't know what the hell you are!

BILL: I'm not a bad person, Joanie.

JOAN: Tell it to the dead girls!

(JOAN pulls the underwear out of her pocket and throws them in BILL's face.)

BILL: Where'd you get those?

JOAN: You tell me.

BILL: It's—it's not what you think.

JOAN: *I found them in your coat pocket!*

BILL: You were going through my pockets?

JOAN: No, no, no, don't think you're gonna turn this around.

BILL: I know you're not going to understand this—

JOAN: If you're having some ridiculous affair with a woman I don't care, but if you're out doing things to girls—to children—to our child?

BILL: God, Joanie, do you think I could do that?

JOAN: You tell me.

BILL: No. I would never—I could never hurt Emily. *(Pause)* This woman—from—

JOAN: *(Covers her ears)* Don't tell me.

BILL: She left them in my car.

JOAN: Before or after?

BILL: After. I know you can't see this—

JOAN: *(Overlapping)* How long? How many times? Once?

BILL: —blinded by your own pain, but I hurt too. *(Beat)* Twice.

JOAN: Fuck you.

BILL: I'll end it. It's over, I'll tell her—

JOAN: Stop talking. Don't say another fucking word.

BILL: I love Emily too. No matter how we feel about each other anymore, we have to remember that we both love her.

(JOAN *stands over* BILL *as he breaks down*)

JOAN: I need some air.

(Lights shift)

(JOAN *addresses the audience,* YOUNG JOAN *is nearby.*)

JOAN: I knew Son of Sam was killing people. Killing girls. But I wasn't scared. Even though the first one was on my birthday. And as the summer wore on there were more shootings. But I had other things on my mind. At my party, this boy, who I was so in love with, asked me to slow dance to Stairway to Heaven. After that, he was always foolin around with me. I had this crazy, scary, happy feeling all summer. He walked me home every night. Then he started acting different. He didn't fool around with me as much. He stopped walking me home and I was on my own. I'd run down one way streets the wrong way. One time this car stopped in the middle of the road and started backing up, following me. I cut through an alley and ran home as fast as I could with a pain my side like somebody stabbed me.

(THE BOY *appears upstage in darkness*)

JOAN: *(Beat)* I was losing him. I knew it. So I came up with a plan. It was all wrapped up in Son of Sam. I thought if maybe this boy thought somebody tried to hurt me, he'd feel sorry for me. He'd feel protective of me again and maybe love me. So, I got a fifth of Jack Daniels, which I drank in an alley. I burned cigarette smoke into my eyes, to make them red. I messed up my hair, ripped my shirt, rolled around in the dirt. I got my girlfriend to help me and I kept sayin, does it look like I'm cryin? Am I cryin enough?

(As JOAN *describes the following,* YOUNG JOAN *appears.* THE BOY *embraces her, at first tenderly, then gradually forcing her to the ground.)*

JOAN: By the time I saw him, I believed it. He came right up to me, all concerned, "Who did this to you? I'll kick his ass." It worked. I delivered myself to him: the perfect little victim.

*(THE BOY *presses himself on top of* YOUNG JOAN *and rapes her, quickly, but brutally.* JOAN *watches silently, curling*

up on the floor. Then, THE BOY *rolls off* YOUNG JOAN, *and exits.* YOUNG JOAN *continues the monologue.)*

YOUNG JOAN: When I got home my mother was watchin T V. I said hi. She said, "Double lock the doors." I ate a donut whole. I went to the bathroom. There were three drops of blood on my underwear. I washed them out in the sink. I smoked a cigarette sitting on the toilet. I threw up the donut. I brushed my teeth and crawled into bed. I threw up again, all over myself and the bed, but I couldn't move. My mother came upstairs, and said, like she suddenly caught me, "Were you drinking?" I breathed Jack Daniels and donut vomit into her face, and said, "No."

JOAN: *(Overlapping)* "No." I curled up in the corner on the floor, till she changed the bed, then I slipped between the clean white sheets burrowing deep into the blankness and went to sleep.

YOUNG JOAN: I slept for a long time. I slept and I slept. I'm not sure I ever woke up.

(After a pause, JOAN *gets up and begins cleaning up the stage, knitting needles, shirts, etc. putting them back into their boxes. She picks up a broom and starts sweeping.)*

(Lights fade)

Scene Ten

(A few weeks later. Daylight. KAREN *is helping* JOAN *pack.* KAREN *takes the broom from* JOAN *and finishes sweeping for her)*

KAREN: Do you need a ride to the airport? I can take you, if you need a ride.

JOAN: No. Thank you, though. Bill's coming to get me on his break. I told him he didn't have to, he said he was coming. I didn't argue.

KAREN: If your mother starts driving your crazy, you can always stay with me.

JOAN: She will.

KAREN: Don't go if it's gonna hurt you.

JOAN: I need to see her, even if it's just for the hug she'll have to give me when I walk in the door. After that I'll figure out what next. Maybe I'll write that book.

KAREN: About Rumpelstilskin?

JOAN: No, a true story. *(Taking the dustpan from* KAREN *dumping it into as trash bag)* You were right about the small-hipped woman.

KAREN: I hate it when I'm right.

JOAN: Me too.

KAREN: *(Pause)* I broke up with what's his name.

JOAN: Why this time?

KAREN: I'm tired of uncertainty.

JOAN: Nothing's ever certain.

KAREN: That's why I'm tired of it. *(Beat)* I never wished for anything bad to happen to you, Joan.

JOAN: *(After a small hesitation)* I know.

KAREN: I was pissed you moved out here. And then I was angry about Emily, I mean, I was so angry at both of you. I'm sorry, that's not fair, but that was—is just because I miss her so much.

JOAN: I know.

KAREN: I don't go around wishing bad luck for my friends.

JOAN: It's a dark time, Karen.

KAREN: Stay here. You might still work things out with Bill. Come back to Pittsburgh. You can stay with me.

JOAN: When I was—Emily's age, I was raped.

KAREN: Oh my god—you never said.

JOAN: I never told anybody. There didn't seem to be any point. I never thought about it—until we moved out here and all this started. When Emily. I kept thinking about Emily, if someone had raped her, what it was like for her. Because I know.

KAREN: I'm sorry—

JOAN: I've got to go home. To name it. Like Rumplestilskin. And then maybe I'll come back to Pittsburgh, to Bill, I don't know, what's next. Except I want to start on the path with my eyes open this time, seeing everything for what it is.

(BILL *enters, surprised to see* KAREN.)

KAREN: I just came by, to say goodbye. That's all. Well, I won't put it off anymore because I'll start bawling, and I'll spare you that.

(KAREN *hugs* JOAN, *who tries to pull away, but* KAREN *holds on to* JOAN *a moment longer.*)

(KAREN *mouths the words, "I love you." She gives* BILL *a nod, then exits.*)

JOAN: *(She stares at him for a long time, then decides.)* I'll be ready to leave in a minute.

(JOAN *gathers the last few things she needs, puts on her coat.* BILL *stands in her way, hands in his pockets.*)

BILL: When Emily was born, I thought, this woman has just given me more that I could ever give her even if I lived for a thousand years. *(He puts something in her hands.)* I found this when we were moving. It was wrapped in tissue paper shoved in the back of a drawer.

(JOAN *unwraps a baby tooth.*)

JOAN: Oh my god…

BILL: I'd forgotten about it till they asked if we had anything. I didn't want to give it to them. I thought if I carried it around, it would work some magic and bring her back.

JOAN: I remember when she lost this. She was so worried about it. She wiggled it for weeks, it seemed like. Then it just popped out at the dinner table. She held it up to me with this look of triumph, like see what I did, and I suddenly felt so sad, like there was no going back now. It's still so white, you would think it would've changed. I can feel just where it would have fit into her mouth.

BILL: You can keep it, if you want.

JOAN: She loved me so unconditionally then. We used to dance in the dining room, I'd move the table and we'd dance to the radio, and she'd smile her gap toothed smile at me while I swung her around, turning and turning and turning. You'd come home and say, "What, no dinner!" And she'd say "You're on your own tonight, me and mommy are dancing." And we'd swing her between us. Her face, I remember, just washed with love.

BILL: I remember.

JOAN: I remember thinking, even then: hold onto this moment.

(BILL *wants to hold her, but stops himself.*)

JOAN: I keep trying to figure out how this happened. Did I do something bad? Did I wish this is some dark part of my heart?

BILL: No, you didn't.

JOAN: Even if I did, when I wasn't looking, in a dream, so much more of me loved her. I only wanted to keep her safe.

BILL: They still might find her. Or, she might come home, she might—

JOAN: No. I don't think so. I think— *(Says it)* —she's dead. I don't feel her anymore. And it's my fault.

BILL: No it isn't.

JOAN: Something I did or didn't do, something I passed on to her. I don't believe things happen for no reason!

BILL: Everything happens for no reason. Because it's fucking chaos out there. We try to go back after and figure out why, and think we got it figured out, but in the moment, nobody can see it coming. Nobody can have the whole picture the whole time. When I'm talking to planes, I can't trust the bastards to make that turn, not to ascend when I say descend. I have no control over whether that pilot's worked too many hours, or if he's hungover. The wake turbulence from a 727, normally just a ripple in the air, nails a rudder the wrong way and sends a 737 full of people nose first into the ground. I can't control *that*. Even after you track all the reasons for it. If we didn't move out here. If we didn't send her to that school. If we didn't— . If I didn't say she could go to that party. How could I forsee all of it? Because the truth is, I don't got the whole picture, Joanie. That's the biggest lie I told you, I never had it. I can only focus on what's moving at me in the moment, just enough to bat it away.

(BILL *pauses, waiting for* JOAN *to forgive him, but she is silent.*)

BILL: I can't predict the future. I can't even promise you I'm never gonna hurt you again, but can you trust me for the next five minutes, and just let me hold you?

(JOAN *lets herself be embraced, and returns the embrace*
slightly, before gently disengaging and stepping away from
him)

(Lights fade/shift.)

JOAN: I don't think we get the whole story. How did
it feel to be Little Red Riding Hood: swallowed up by
something dark and dank and then yanked out at the
last minute, slimy and dazed, blinking in the too bright
sun? Did she have nightmares afterwards? Or did she
forget? And what was it like to be Little Red Riding
Hood's mother? Of course, she was overwhelmed
by *guilt*. And did the Grandmother ever take
responsibility for her part in it? That woodcutter, he's
the wildcard isn't he? If he wasn't there to cut open the
wolf and pull them out just in the knick of time. Now,
if I were writing this story, all the woodcutter would
be able to salvage would be her pearly milk tooth.
And one day, after the pain of longing for her child,
nearly splits Little Red's Mother in two, she dreams
that she swallows that little tooth, like a hard bright
seed, hoping to choke on it. But instead of dying,
she transforms into something graceful and hooved,
with dark liquid eyes that sense movement before it
happens, that breathes fear gladly, because that's what
keeps her alive. And should the woodcutter look out
his window at just the right moment, he wouldn't see
her running past, because she's already gone. *(She*
places the tooth in her mouth.)

Scene Eleven

(JOAN *is outside, walking into the woods. She sees something on the ground and freezes.* EMILY *appears by her side. She is very young*)

EMILY: What is it?

JOAN: It looks like a, some kind of, uh, animal.

EMILY: What's wrong with it?

JOAN: Well, it looks like maybe it's slee— (*Stops before saying "sleeping"*) Slowed down. *Don't touch it!*

EMILY: It's dead, isn't it?

JOAN: It's not alive anymore, no.

EMILY: It's a dead rabbit! Why don't you say so?

JOAN: I don't want to scare you.

EMILY: I'd be afraid if it was alive. It could bite me.

JOAN: Rabbits don't bite.

EMILY: They have teeth. They could bite. Can I take it home?

JOAN: No, leave it.

EMILY: I want the fur.

JOAN: No, Emily, don't touch it, let's go.

EMILY: You're afraid of it.

JOAN: I'm not afraid, it's just, it's dead, it could be diseased.

EMILY: (*Staring at rabbit, then a realization*) Are you going to die?

JOAN: (*Kneeling down to face her*) Yes, yes, I am, but not for a long long time and you'll be a woman with a husband to take care of you, I mean who you will take care of, what I mean is, you will take care of each other. And you'll have children of your own. That you will

both take care of. Or maybe you'll have a job. Whatever
you want, but you'll be grown up.

EMILY: Am I going to die?

JOAN: Not until you've lived a long time and your
children are grown up and they have children. And
you'll tell them stories about taking walks in Schenley
Park with your mother picking wildflowers.

EMILY: So everybody dies.

JOAN: Yes.

EMILY: And then what?

JOAN: Hm. Well. I want to say you go to heaven.

EMILY: What's heaven?

JOAN: *(Says with* EMILY *simultaneously)* What's heaven?
Yeah. I knew that was next. It's, well, where God is.

EMILY: You mean we go to church?

JOAN: Nobody really knows where heaven is exactly.
Some people believe it's high above the sky.

EMILY: *(Skeptical, precocious)* I find that hard to believe.

JOAN: I believe that God is the part of us that loves each
other. When we die, we go there, and our bodies are
left behind to turn into something else. Like, the rabbit.
Someday, its body might turn into... wildflowers.

EMILY: So...I'll be a wildflower?

JOAN: Maybe.

EMILY: Okay.

JOAN: Let's keep walking, Emily. How about I tell you
a story...

(JOAN walks, holding EMILY's *hand, but* EMILY *is rooted to
the spot.)*

EMILY: We should cover her. The rabbit.

JOAN: *(Looks at* EMILY, *nods)* Get some leaves. And some sticks.

EMILY: And some flowers…

(JOAN *and* EMILY *gather some leaves, sticks, etc, and kneel down in front of the rabbit, covering it gently, as lights fade.)*

END OF PLAY